SO-AKL-472

EXPLORING WORLD CULTURES

United States

Sharon Gordon

Cavendish Square

New York

To my beautiful granddaughters, Isabelle Rose and Grace Mackenzie, and to my first grandson, yet unborn. And to my parents who, despite a lack of wealth, gave their five children a truly rich upbringing.

Published in 2016 by Cavendish Square Publishing, LLC
243 5th Avenue, Suite 136, New York, NY 10016

First Edition

Website: cavendishsq.com

This publication represents the opinions and views of the author based on his or her personal experience, knowledge, and research. The information in this book serves as a general guide only. The author and publisher have used their best efforts in preparing this book and disclaim liability rising directly or indirectly from the use and application of this book.

CPSIA Compliance Information: Batch #WS15CSQ

All websites were available and accurate when this book was sent to press.

Library of Congress Cataloging-in-Publication Data

Gordon, Sharon.
United States / Sharon Gordon.
pages cm. — (Exploring world cultures)
Includes index.
ISBN 978-1-50260-577-1 (hardcover) ISBN 978-1-50260-576-4 (paperback) ISBN 978-1-50260-578-8 (ebook)
1. United States—Juvenile literature. I. Title.
E156.G673 2015
973—dc23

2014046813

Editorial Director: David McNamara
Editor: Kristen Susienka
Copy Editor: Cynthia Roby
Art Director: Jeffrey Talbot
Designer: Joseph Macri
Senior Production Manager: Jennifer Ryder-Talbot
Production Editor: Renni Johnson
Photo Research: J8 Media

The photographs in this book are used by permission and through the courtesy of: KidStock/Getty Images, cover; Wavebreakmedia/Shutterstock, 5; File:Usa edcp (+HI +AL) relief location map.svg/Wikimedia Commons, 6; The Frick Collection, New York, File:George Washington by Gilbert Stuart, 1795-96.png /Wikimedia Commons, 8; Chip Somodevilla/Getty Images, 11; Majeczka/Shutterstock, 13; Spwidoff/Sjutterstock, 15; John Birdsall/AGE Fotostock, 16; Mitchell Funk/Getty Images, 18; Harold M. Lambert/Kean Collection/Archive Photos/Getty Images, 20; Btrenkel/Getty Images, 22; Bebeto Matthews/AP Photo, 25; David E. Klutho /Sports Illustrated/Getty Images, 26; Etitarenko/Shutterstock, 28.

Printed in the United States of America

Contents

Introduction

The United States is a unique country. It offers freedom to people who live there. It has welcomed new people throughout its history. Today, many new immigrants come to live in the United States because they like the lifestyle.

Many people in the United States have a good life. Their homes are warm in the winter. They can see a doctor when they are sick. There is food on the table. The poor can get help for their basic needs. People live longer than ever before.

The United States is a powerful nation. Men and women in the military are trained to protect the people. They help out when sudden dangers occur around the world. They bring supplies to people in need.

Most areas of the country enjoy the four different seasons. There are colorful leaves in fall, soft snowflakes in winter, bright colors in spring, and warm days in summer.

Many people want to come to the United States and few people want to leave.

This young girl holds the flag of the United States.

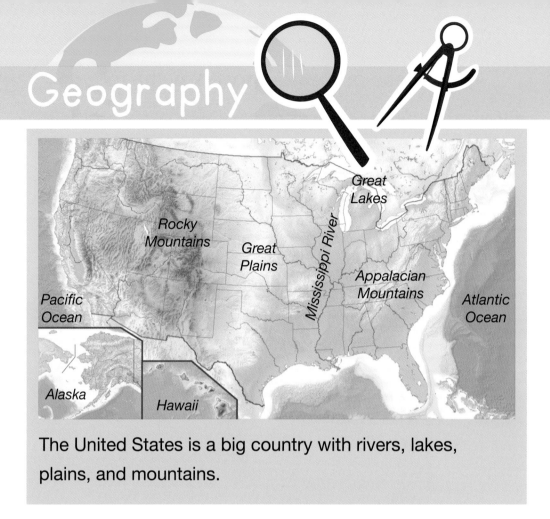

The United States is a big country with rivers, lakes, plains, and mountains.

The United States is the world's fourth-largest country. It is made up of fifty states. Two of the states, Alaska and Hawaii, do not touch the rest.

The Atlantic Ocean is on the eastern coast. The Pacific Ocean is on the western coast. The Mississippi River runs down the middle. Oceans and rivers are important to the country. Ships sail into the ports.

The Great Lakes

These five lakes are a part of the border with Canada.

Generally, the United States has a good climate. Northern states have longer winters and short, mild summers. Southern states are warm most of the year.

In the western states are the great Rocky Mountains. Arizona's Grand Canyon has steep rocks. The Appalachian Mountains are in the east. In between are open, grassy areas called the Great Plains.

FACT!

Ocean water on the East Coast is warmer than that on the West Coast. The **Gulf Stream** brings up warm water from sunny Florida.

The United States became a country on July 4, 1776. It had thirteen states. George Washington was the first president.

This painting of George Washington hangs in the Frick Museum in New York City.

The United States quickly grew in land and people. Roads and bridges were built. New states were added. However, there was a problem. The southern states had slaves while the northern states did not. The North and South went to war in 1861. When the North won the Civil War

In 1848, gold was found in California. Two years later, California became the thirty-first state.

in 1865, President Abraham Lincoln freed the slaves.

In the 1900s, the United States fought in two World Wars. In between came the Great Depression. Many people lost their jobs. Banks were closed.

Today, the United States is a world leader. It helps bring freedom to other nations.

9/11

On September 11, 2001, terrorists flew airplanes into important buildings in New York City. This began the War on Terror.

The United States has a three-part government system. Each part of government is described in the **Constitution**. It was written in 1787 and describes the basic laws of the United States.

- Legislative branch: Congress (House of Representatives and the Senate) writes new laws and votes on which laws to pass.

The United States Congress meets to listen to a world leader.

- Judicial branch: Made up of the courts. This branch decides if laws break the rules of the Constitution. The highest court is the Supreme Court.

- Executive branch: The president, vice president, and the vice president's cabinet make sure laws are followed. The president can say "no" to a law that Congress passes.

All citizens eighteen years and older can vote. Each state has one representative and two senators in Congress. They speak for the people.

Bill of Rights

The Bill of Rights was added to the Constitution. It lists ten important freedoms.

The Economy

The United States is a rich nation. It has the largest **economy** in the world. It buys and sells more goods than any other country. There are many jobs for its workers.

The Stock Market

The stock market in New York City manages **stocks**. If the value goes up, people make money. If the value goes down, people lose money.

Farmers sell their crops. Businesses make cars and clothing. Builders make homes and offices. Factories make planes.

FACT!

All coins are made at the United States Mint. Many people like to collect them.

These wind turbines use wind to make electricity.

Important materials are in the earth and air. Coal comes from **mines** deep underground. Rigs bring up oil from the earth. Natural gas is piped underground. The sun, wind, and water are all used to make electricity.

Many jobs are about helping others. Hospital workers take care of the sick. Teachers help students learn. Chefs at restaurants make delicious food.

13

The Environment

The environment is important to all living things. People, plants, and animals need clean air and water.

Endangered Species Act

Congress keeps a list of plants and animals that are in danger. This list is called the Endangered Species Act. It protects the places where animals live.

In the past, people were not careful with items they threw out. Many lakes and rivers were polluted. Fish could not live in them. Dirty smoke from cars and factories filled the air.

Today, people in homes and businesses follow new rules to help keep the environment clean. They recycle their paper, cans, and bottles.

Recycling helps keep the environment clean.

Trees and forests are good for the environment. They help make the air safe to breathe. Wetlands are home to many animals and birds. They make nests near the water. Workers test to see if the water is safe.

FACT!

The United States has 401 different parks. The National Park Service takes care of them all.

The United States has the third-largest population in the world: 316 million people. Only China and India have more people.

People from many different countries call the United States their home.

People have always come to the United States for freedom. They can choose where to live and where to work. They can choose to marry or not.

In the past, people came from Europe. Today, the country has many races from all over the world. California has the most people of all the states. Many **Latinos** live there.

Most people like to live in or near big cities. Their friends and jobs are close. Some people like the country, where there is open space. Many older people like the warmth of Florida.

FACT!

Some areas of cities are known to have many people living there. Chinatown in New York City has a population of 150,000 people.

Lifestyle

Family life is very important to the people of the United States. Children need good schools. Families enjoy neighborhood parks and playgrounds.

Central Park in New York City is a popular place.

For those who live near cities, it is easy to get around. Transportation, such as subways, buses, taxis, trains, and planes, takes people from one place to another.

FACT!

Central Park in New York City is a beautiful place to walk, ride bikes, or picnic. It even has a zoo.

Both men and women enjoy their jobs. On weekends, many families enjoy a good meal together. On weekdays, children attend school and study with friends.

Women in the United States have become more involved in areas of society that they once could not join. They run for office. They are business leaders. They find time to care for their children and older parents.

Susan B. Anthony

Susan B. Anthony helped women have the right to vote and own property.

Religion

The earliest **settlers** were Christians. They crossed the Atlantic Ocean in search of religious freedom. They did not want the government telling them what to believe.

The Pilgrims crossed the Atlantic Ocean to find religious freedom.

Today that idea is still important. All religions are welcome in the United States.

Christianity is the most popular religion. Some Christians are Roman Catholic and some are Protestant. They meet in churches. People in the South go to church more regularly than those in other parts of the country.

There are many other religions, too. Jewish people worship in synagogues. Buddhists worship in temples. Muslims worship in mosques.

Native Americans

Native American religions believe in a Great Spirit. They believe there is a good life after death.

Some people are called atheists. They choose to not join any religion. In the United States, it is okay to practice any religion you choose, or not.

FACT!

Yoga has become popular in the United States. It helps people quiet their minds and relax their bodies.

Although the United States has no official language, English has always been most common. Spanish is the second most popular. After that, many Asian languages are spoken. In many homes, two languages often are spoken.

In addition to English, many students learn to speak other languages, like Chinese.

English is an important world language. Students in other countries learn English in school. They want to be able to talk to business leaders from the United States.

Different Words, Same Language

Over time, new words are added to English. We have "nachos" from Mexico, "café" from France, and "texting" because of cell phones.

English sounds different from one place to another. People have different ways of saying the same thing. People from the South might say, "Hey, y'all," instead of "Hello, everyone." Some people call soft drinks "soda" and others call it "pop." Many people living in Boston would call their hometown "BAAH-ston."

FACT!

People who cannot hear or speak use sign language. They speak with their hands.

Arts and Festivals

In the United States, people young and old enjoy the **arts**. Every year there are many festivals and performances. Children take part in school plays and choirs.

Juilliard

The Juilliard School is a top arts school for dance, acting, and music.

Concerts are very popular in the United States. Fans enjoy seeing their favorite musicians in person.

New York City is the center for all kinds of arts. It is home to many famous art museums. People love to go to Broadway shows. The Rockettes are known for their show *Radio City Christmas Spectacular*.

People attend Brooklyn's Cherry Blossom Festival.

Flower festivals are held each year in the spring. Beautiful cherry blossoms brighten Washington, DC. The Philadelphia Flower Show is the largest indoor flower show in the world. The largest tulip festival in the United States is held each year in Holland, Michigan.

FACT!

A big parade for Mardi Gras, or Fat Tuesday, is held in New Orleans, Louisiana, every year. People wear masks and costumes.

There is a lot to do for fun in the United States. Many people ride bikes or play sports. Soccer, baseball, and basketball are very popular. Adults and children love to go to sports games.

Baseball brings thousands of fans to the ballpark.

Families enjoy vacations. They go to the beach or hike in the mountains. They camp in a park or fish in a lake.

Millions of families visit Disney World in Florida each year.

Many people try to get exercise every day. They walk or jog around their neighborhood, or go to a local gym.

Indoor malls fill up on rainy days. On the weekends, friends go out to see movies or watch them at home. There are books to read and crafts to make.

Parades are held on many holidays. The Fourth of July has parades and fireworks. Mardi Gras is held in New Orleans each year. Big Thanksgiving Day and St. Patrick's Day parades are held in New York City.

You can find all kinds of food in the United States. A traditional meal might be meat with potatoes and vegetables. Today, people from different countries make their own special foods. There are Greek and Italian restaurants. Sushi is a popular Japanese dish. Fast food restaurants serve pizza, tacos, and chicken. Diners are open for breakfast, lunch, and dinner.

Watermelon is a healthy food to eat in the summer.

FACT!

Philadelphia made the Philly cheesesteak sandwich in the 1930s. It is now popular all across the United States.

Families love to have summer picnics. They grill hot dogs and hamburgers. They make salads and desserts. Watermelon tastes good with everything. So do ice cream and cupcakes.

More and more, people try to eat healthy foods, such as fresh fruits and vegetables. Some like organic food. Some eat only vegetables. Farmers markets sell good, locally grown food.

Chuck Wagon

Chuck wagons were used by cowboys traveling with food. They kept it in a "chuck box."

Glossary

arts A category that defines enjoyment of music, theater, dance, or drama.

Constitution The basic laws of the United States.

economy The process or system by which goods and services are produced, sold, and bought in a country or region.

Gulf Stream Warm air that moves from the Gulf of Mexico to the upper United States.

Latinos A native or inhabitant of Latin America.

mines Holes dug by people to go underground and search for objects such as coal or diamonds.

settlers People who make a new area—typically one with no or few people—their home.

stocks A type of security, or proof, that means ownership in a corporation.

Find Out More

Books

Hintz, Martin. *United States of America*. New York: Children's Press, 2004.

Scillian, Devin. *A Is for America*. Chelsea, MI: Sleeping Bear Press, 2001.

Websites

The Animated Atlas

www.animatedatlas.com

The United States Geological Survey for Kids

education.usgs.gov/primary.html

Videos

History Videos

kids.usa.gov/watch-videos/history/index.shtml
Watch any of these history videos and develop a better understanding about life in the United States, yesterday and today.

Index

About the Author

Sharon Gordon has been writing children's books for many years. She has written science and nature books. Born and raised in the United States, her parents and grandparents were poor Dutch immigrants who left Holland to start a new life. For fun, Sharon likes to travel. When she is not writing, she loves spending time with her family.